PUPPETS

• CONTENTS •

A Read-about

• WRITTEN BY ALAN TRUSSELL-CULLEN •

The History of Puppets

People have been making puppets for centuries. Puppet-like dolls made by the ancient Egyptians have been found in the pyramids, and there is evidence of even earlier puppets in China and India.

We know that the ancient Greeks and Romans loved their puppet shows too. In the year 422BC, a rich Greek nobleman named Callia gave a great dinner to show off his wealth. But the big attraction for the guests was not the food and wine. What everyone enjoyed most was the puppet show provided for their entertainment.

Puppets have always been popular in the East too. In fact, some people believe that the first puppet shows originated in India and were brought to Europe by gypsies.

In China, for hundreds of years, strolling puppet-masters wandered through the countryside, performing their glove puppet plays to interested villagers and townsfolk.

PUNCH & JUDY

Some puppet plays are very old too. Everyone knows about *Mr Punch* and his wife *Judy.* But other Punch-like puppets exist in different parts of Europe. Italian children love to cheer on their puppet favourite *Pulcinella,* while German children will tell you about *Kaspar.* In Russia there is another impish puppet just like Punch called *Petrouchka.*

Puppets of Today

Fifty years ago, puppet shows were common sights at fairs and on the beaches in summer. Today traditional puppet shows are harder to find.

Some professional puppeteers travel round from school to school, presenting their puppet plays and helping children to make their own puppets. Some puppeteers perform their shows at children's parties and in shopping malls where they amuse the children while their parents go off to do some shopping.

But the place where you are most likely to see puppets nowadays is on television. The "Thunderbird" puppets were very popular in the 1970s.

But perhaps the most successful puppets on television have been the Muppets. The American puppeteer, Jim Henson, created the Muppets for the educational programme "Sesame Street". Characters like Big Bird, Kermit the Frog and Miss Piggy soon had a huge following. It wasn't long before these television "stars" were demanding a show of their own. The result was "The Muppet Show", now shown in countries round the world.

Did you know...

The ancient Chinese puppet masters made "powder puppets". These puppets, powered by gun powder, were a kind of fireworks puppet.

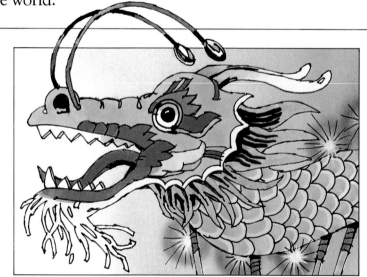

Finger Puppets

Puppets are doll-like people or animals. The puppeteer brings them to life by moving and using them to tell stories.

Puppets come in all shapes and sizes. Some puppets are so small they can fit on the end of your finger.

You can easily make a finger puppet. Just draw a face on your finger tip with a ballpoint pen. Draw two faces and you have two puppets ready to talk to each other.

You can also make finger puppets out of matchboxes, egg cartons, toilet roll tubes, and small packets or paper bags.

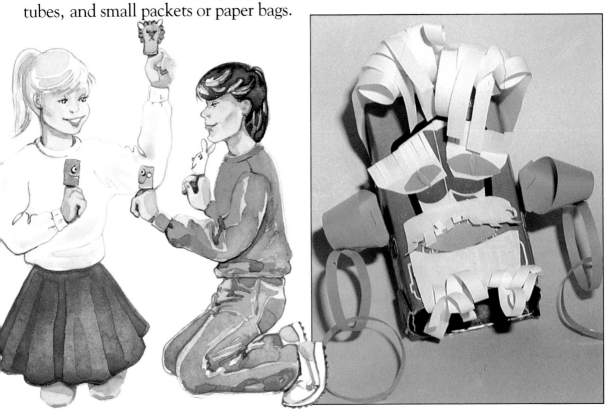

Glove Puppets

Glove puppets are larger than finger puppets and are worked by wearing them on your hand like a glove.

You can make a simple glove puppet by using marker pens to draw mouth and eyes onto an old light-coloured sock. Some strands of knitting yarn will make excellent hair.

You can also make glove puppets out of empty packets and paper bags.

Did you know. . .

Punch's wife wasn't always called Judy. A few hundred years ago, she was called Joan so audiences in those days went to see a "Punch and Joan" show!

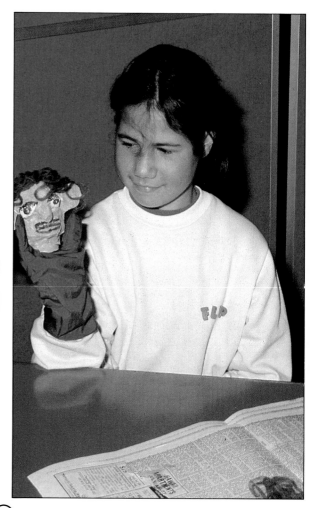

Making a Papier Mâché Puppet

MATERIALS:

CARDBOARD TUBE
from inside a toilet paper roll.

NEWSPAPER
torn into thin strips.

WALLPAPER PASTE,
enough to fill a bucket.

WOOLLEN KNITTING YARN
or cotton wool for hair.

CLOTH, NEEDLE, THREAD
to make clothes. Add buttons for decoration.

POSTER PAINTS AND PAINT BRUSH
to paint the puppet's face.

METHOD:

Shred newspaper. Place in bucket of wallpaper paste. Leave to soak. Prepare a ball of dry newspaper. Push in the toilet roll neck-tube and hold in place with tape. Paste paper strips over paper ball until whole head is covered with strips. Model chin, nose, etc.

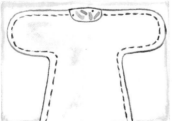

When the head is dry, paint on a face. You could also varnish your puppet head when the paint is dry. Sew together back and front of body, glue to neck tube. Add buttons and hair.

Making a Stage for Glove Puppets

A large cardboard carton such as a refrigerator carton or a washing machine carton makes a great theatre. Cut a rectangular hole high in one side for your stage opening. Cut a large hole low down in the opposite side so you can get into the box. Kneel in the carton and raise your puppet-hands so your audience can see them performing through the stage opening. Paint the outside of your theatre in bright colours. If you like, you can paint scenery on the back wall of your theatre.

Did you know...

The famous French puppeteer Laurent Mourguet actually began his puppet career in 1793 as a toothpuller! He used a little puppet called Polichinelle to attract customers to his toothpulling booth in the market.

Rod  Puppets

A rod puppet is worked from below like a glove puppet, but it is held up by rods of wood or stiff wire.

Glove puppets can only be as big as your hand, but rod puppets can be as large as you like. In fact, if you want to, you could make a rod puppet as large as a fully grown person!

A Simple Rod Puppet to Make

MATERIALS:

AN OLD BROOM
the sort illustrated, with short bristles and a wooden head.

CHILDREN'S CLOTHES
an old shirt and a pair of long pants.

THREE PIECES OF DOWEL
of wood or plastic, long enough to operate head and arms from behind stage.

A CUPHOOK OR EYEHOOK
with a loop large enough for the main dowel to slide through.

PAPER BAG
for puppet's head. Choose a bag the right size for the rest of his body.

NEWSPAPER
enough to stuff the head and the body.

METHOD:

1 Draw or paint a face on the paper bag and stuff with crumpled newspaper.

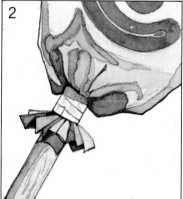

2 Using tape, attach head to end of one length of dowel.

3 Sew up cuff ends of shirt and trousers, then sew waist of shirt into waistband of pants.

4

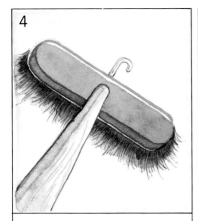

Screw the cuphook into the top middle edge of the broom head.

5

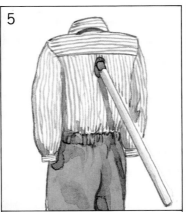

Place broom inside shirt with broom handle sticking out through back of shirt. (Make a hole in the shirt back if necessary.)

6

Slide the dowel with the head on it down through the cuphook and out the same hole in the back of the shirt.

7

Stuff the clothes with crumpled newspaper and secure to broom handle beneath head.

Tie the remaining dowels to the ends of your puppet's sleeves.

Now your puppet is ready to work!

You will need three people to work your puppet – one to hold the broom handle and work the head rod, and one to control each of the arms. If your puppet is going to "speak", you may need a fourth person to read the puppet's lines.

Marionettes

Marionettes are puppets with jointed arms and legs. Their movements are controlled by strings fastened to various parts of the body — to hands, feet, head, neck, knees, elbows, to anything that the puppet-master wants to make move. The strings are attached to a control handle which enables the puppet-master to make the puppet move in all manner of ways.

Making a 3-string Marionette

MATERIALS:

A PING-PONG OR
POLYSTYRENE BALL
for the marionette's head.

A SMALL PIECE OF WOOD
about 20cm x 2cm x .5 for
control handle.

NEEDLE AND THREAD
to stitch your puppet
together.

CARDBOARD SCRAPS
to make hands and feet.

A SQUARE OF CLOTH
or a man's handkerchief.

MARKER PENS
to draw puppet's face on ping-
pong ball.

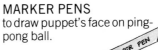

Draw a face on the head of your puppet.

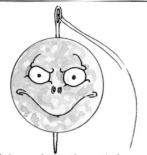

Using a long thread, force the needle down through the top of the ball head and out the other side. Leave lots of thread at the top.

Fold the cloth diagonally to make a triangle. Sew the "neck" end of the thread into the middle of the fold, knot it and remove the needle.

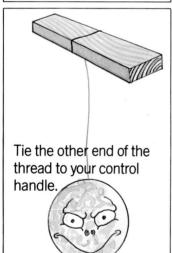

Tie the other end of the thread to your control handle.

Make cardboard hands and feet and staple them onto the cloth. The hands will go at each end of the long fold, the feet at the two lower hanging corners.

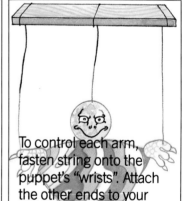

To control each arm, fasten string onto the puppet's "wrists". Attach the other ends to your control handle.

Your puppet is now ready for you to bring it to life!

For finishing touches you could glue some yarn to the head of your marionette for hair and add features of buttons or bows to its body.

Shadow Puppets

Shadow Puppets are fun too. Try "making" these shadow puppets with your hands. Stand between a bright light source (such as a slide projector) and a plain-coloured wall.

But you can also make shadow puppets with a screen.

Tape some thin paper to a window where the sun is shining in and work these simple cardboard puppets from outside the room. Your audience watches from inside the room.

Shadow puppets are usually made from flat cardboard cut-outs. Thin sticks or wires are fastened to the puppets so they can be moved to cast shadows on a screen.

Use thin paper for the screen — waxed paper, used for cooking, is excellent for this. To keep it tight and free from wrinkles, attach the paper with tape to the legs of an upturned desk or small table. For light, use a reading lamp or slide projector. Place the light so it shines on the back of the screen. You work the puppets from behind the screen while the audience watches from in front of the screen.

Another good way to show shadow puppet plays is to place your puppets on top of an overhead projector so they can be shone onto a screen or wall.

All sorts of things can be done to make your shadow plays more interesting.

You can tape-record the words spoken by your puppets so you can concentrate on getting their movements right.

Interesting effects can be achieved by using coloured cellophane too. Cellophane by itself is not easy to handle but you can cut out sections of your puppets and paste cellophane over these holes. You could make a house as part of your scenery. Cut out the window openings and paste yellow cellophane over these. Prop the house against the back of your screen so the light shines to show the dark shadowy shape of the house with its cheerfully glowing windows.

Presenting Your Own Puppet Play

You can easily turn popular stories like "Goldilocks and the Three Bears" or "The Three Billy Goats Gruff" into puppet plays. Or make up your own puppet stories and write and present your own puppet plays to your family and friends. Here is a little puppet play you might like to try too.

Mr Punch:

HEAD:

Make this from papier mâché. (Look back at page 7.) Make his nose and chin quite large. Model these from extra smaller balls of paper and hold them in place with thin pasted strips. Paint the head when it is dry.

HAT:

The picture shows you what the hat should look like; it could even be made from an old sock! Sew or glue it to the head.

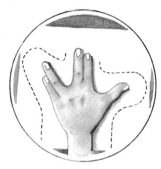

GLOVE BODY:

Make a paper pattern by tracing round your hand. Spread your fingers as shown but make the pattern bigger all round so the glove fits loosely. Your two smaller fingers and your thumb will become the arms. Your two middle fingers will be the neck. Make your glove wrong side out. Pin your pattern onto your material and cut round it. Sew round the outer edges. Leave the bottom open for your hand to go in. Shorten the glove-neck and leave it open for your two middle fingers to poke through. Turn the glove right side out. Hide the join at the bottom of the neck with a collar or bow tie and because Mr Punch is a waiter he could also be wearing an apron.

Lady Customer:

HEAD:

Make her head from papier mâché. Try to make it look different from Mr Punch's. You could make her hair from cotton wool or strands of knitting yarn. Will you put a ribbon in her hair? Will she have an unusual hat? Earrings perhaps?

CLOTHES:

Make a glove as you did for Mr Punch, but use a different coloured material. You could sew some big buttons down the front of her dress. Give her a coloured scarf or perhaps a shawl round her shoulders. Two or three strings of papier mâché beads round her neck would make her look attractive too.

Props:

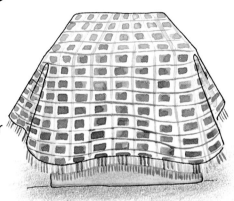

TABLE:

Fasten a small box to the front of the stage. To make a table cloth, cut out a square of fabric large enough to cover the whole box and glue it in place.

SOUP BOWL:

Use a doll's bowl or a small glass or see-through bowl. Real soup would spill so half fill it with small pieces of cellophane which will look like soup.

SPIDER:

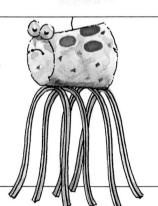

To make its long dangly legs, cut four big rubber bands in half to make eight legs and attach them to a cork body with glue. If you want to give your spider some feelers, poke two plastic-headed pins into his head. Paint your spider bright gaudy colours.

FLY:

Use a cork or a small polystyrene ball for your fly's body. Cut a pipe cleaner into three even lengths and poke these into the body for legs. Use pins for eyes and cut out two triangles from stiff plastic and glue these onto your fly's back for its wings.

Stage:

A large cardboard carton makes a good stage. Cut out one side and glue back the flaps. Paint your backdrop and attach curtains to a string across the front. Hang a curtain or blanket in front of your stage to hide your puppeteers.

(WOMAN CUSTOMER SITTING AT CARDBOARD TABLE WAITING TO BE SERVED.)

- CUSTOMER: Waiter! Waiter! I've been sitting here for half an hour!

- PUNCH:
  (ENTERING, HOLDING MENU.)
  Coming, Madam! Coming, Madam! Half an hour, you say? You're lucky. Our last customer was here a week before anyone noticed! What would you like to eat today?

- CUSTOMER: I'd like the menu, please!

- PUNCH: And how would you like it? Boiled? Roasted? Or fried?

- CUSTOMER: I want to read it!

- PUNCH: Of course! Of course! There we are!

- CUSTOMER: I'll have the roast lamb, thank you.

- PUNCH: Sorry. It's off. *

- CUSTOMER: Then I'll have the beef.

- PUNCH: That's off too.

- CUSTOMER: What about the pork?

- PUNCH: That's really off!

- CUSTOMER: Then what can I have?

- PUNCH: How about soup of the day?

- CUSTOMER: What day is it?

- PUNCH: Hold on. I'll check.
  (HE GOES OFF AND COMES BACK WITH A BOWL.)

- PUNCH: Here it is. It's Thursday's.

- CUSTOMER: But today's Tuesday!

- PUNCH: Eat it quickly. That way you don't get to taste it!

- CUSTOMER: Waiter!

- PUNCH: What's the matter now, Madam?

- CUSTOMER: There's a fly in my soup!

*Off the menu and "off" in freshness

- PUNCH: Sh! Don't shout about it – everyone will want one!

- CUSTOMER: Look! It's a dead fly!

- PUNCH: I know. It's the heat that kills them.

- CUSTOMER: And it's only got three legs!

- PUNCH: Don't worry, Madam. The Cook will find you the other three.

- CUSTOMER: This is preposterous! I can't possibly eat soup with a fly in it!

- PUNCH: Just a minute, Madam. I'll fix it for you.
  (PUNCH GOES OUT.)

CUSTOMER: Hey! Where are you going?

PUNCH:
(RETURNING WITH BIG SPIDER.)
Coming, Madam!
(HE DROPS THE SPIDER INTO THE SOUP.)
There!

CUSTOMER: What did you put in my soup?

PUNCH: A spider, Madam.

CUSTOMER: A what?

PUNCH: Well, the spider can eat the fly and you can eat the soup!

CUSTOMER: This is too much! I'm leaving!

PUNCH: Wait! Wait! What about my tip?

CUSTOMER: You want a tip after this appalling service?

PUNCH: I wouldn't say no. . .

CUSTOMER: All right! I'll give you a tip! But first you must sit down at the table and close your eyes.

PUNCH: Close my eyes?

CUSTOMER: Yes. I want it to be a big surprise.

PUNCH: Oh, goodie! I love surprises!
(HE PUTS HANDS OVER EYES.)
My eyes are closed. Oh, I do hope it'll be a nice big tip!

● CUSTOMER:
(PICKS UP SOUP BOWL.)
It'll be a big tip all right! And here it is!
(SHE POURS BOWL OVER PUNCH.)

● PUNCH: Help! Help! I can't swim!

● CUSTOMER: Serves you right! I'll never come here again!

(PUNCH TASTES SOUP.)

● PUNCH: I say. . . this soup. . .

● CUSTOMER: What about it?

● PUNCH:
(TASTES SOME MORE. SMACKS LIPS.)
It's delicious!

● CUSTOMER: Delicious?

● PUNCH: I'm going to ask the Chef for some more! Bye. . .
(PUNCH GOES OFF. CUSTOMER STARES AS HE GOES, THEN COLLAPSES IN AMAZEMENT.)

● CUSTOMER: Aaaah. . .!